Dear Ryan,

No Wheelchairs in *Heaven*

Jesus Came To Restore Our Inheritance

Much love + A few
♥♥
hugs.

Meredith Moyer

Meredith

allison + my
journey
& ♥ heart.

xulon
PRESS

www.xulonpress.com

At the tender age of 8

Allison prayed a humble prayer asking Jesus to help her, forgive her, and come into her heart... so she could have what He offers the gift of eternal life.

At the age of 29

I whispered in her ear "Ali, it's alright. Run home to Heaven, right into the loving arms of Jesus.
Give Him the biggest kiss, and one day soon I will be running right behind." Before I could stand up straight she left - without a labored breath... kissing her wheel-chair goodbye.

This book was written in her honor.

Table of Contents

Forward by Dr. Don Schoendorfer xi

Chapter 1 - A Letter to my Daughter 15

Chapter 2 - Made In God's Image 24

Chapter 3 - Kissing Her Wheelchair Goodbye 30

Chapter 4 - Before You Were Born 38

Chapter 5 - What Went Wrong 45

Chapter 6 - Jesus Got It Back 54

Chapter 7 - Jesus Words of Comfort 59

Chapter 8 - Friends Sharing Memories 65

Acknowledgments

I wrote this as a grateful memorial to a Heavenly Father who is a master planner, designer, and giver of all life. We are made by Him and for Him with a precious uniqueness that is priceless, irreplaceable. It is His story that we have been born into, which leads to eternal life, and the longing for a place we have never seen: *Heaven.*

> *"The God who made the world and everything in it is the Lord of Heaven and earth. From one man He made every nation of men that they would inhabit the whole earth; and He determined the times set for them and the exact places where they should live. God did this so that men would seek Him and perhaps reach out for Him and find Him, though He is not far from each one of us. For it is in Him, that we live and move and have our being."*

Acts 17:24-28

I extend my most sincere gratitude to the hundreds of wonderful people who supported Allison's world in numerous ways – including family members, the Bellingham and Lynden School Districts, the medical community, our local churches, and advocacy communities across the state. Her world was enriched by each and every one of you. It brings a smile to know that, to name everyone, I would need to write another book. I thank you for the lessons you taught, your love, laughter, affection and compassionate care.

You will never know how you blessed us by your presence.

Forward

I remember back several years ago when I first had the opportunity to meet Meredith Moyer and her daughter, Allison. The two women had become aware of Free Wheelchair Mission's work in providing mobility to the poor in developing countries, and decided they wanted to help. They began to fundraise through their church and among their community of family and friends and were very successful. Supporters of World Vision, they decided to link our two organizations, and we all met for the first time in World Vision's national headquarters in Federal Way, Washington. Meredith had arranged to present FWM with a check for the funds they raised for wheelchairs during World Vision's weekly chapel service.

I addressed the gathering first, speaking about Free Wheelchair Mission and the global need for mobility, but anything I might have said fell into the shadows when

Allison was wheeled to the podium. Her condition was quite advanced at that point, and she struggled to speak; the chapel held its breath as the young woman voiced a question that would move the crowd far more than I could ever hope to do.

"What would my life be like if I had no wheelchair?"

Eleven words. It was all she had to say. I looked around the room. I could see the audience considering her few spare words, trying to imagine how Allison would survive without mobility, how much harder her mother would have had to struggle, how difficult the challenge to provide a beloved child with a taste of all that life has to offer. Eyes filled with dampness, and tears fell. Eleven words. All it took to change hearts and lift hopes and raise thoughts to God's grace.

In my few moments with this inspirational young woman, I was reminded not just of the obstacles we face, the struggles that disability creates and the importance of mobility for all, but of the strength of the human spirit. Allison reminded us that the essence of our humanity is found not within the limits of our fragile bodies, but in our eternal connection to spirit, and our shared compassion and responsibility for all God's children. I will never forget her.

Dr. Don Schoendorfer
Founder and President of the
Free Wheelchair Mission
www.FreeWheelchairMission.org

Free Wheelchair Mission distributes light weight wheelchairs to the impoverished disabled in developing nations. The Congressional Medal of Honor Society presented Don with the Above & Beyond Citizens award in March 2008 for His Humanitarian work. With the ministry of Jesus Christ as their inspiration, Free Wheelchair Mission has delivered over 540,550 wheelchairs in over 76 countries.

Proceeds from book will be donated to Free Wheelchair Mission.

Chapter 1

A Letter to My Daughter

*The Lord Jesus Christ...will transform our lowly
bodies so that they will be like his glorious body.*

Philippians 3:20-21

*Somewhere in my broken, paralyzed body is the seed
of what I shall become. The paralysis makes what I am
to become all the more grand when you contrast atro-
phied, useless legs against splendorous resurrected
legs. I'm convinced that if there are mirrors in Heaven
(and why not?), the image I'll see will be unmistakably
"Joni," although a much better, brighter Joni. So much
so that it's not worth comparing...I will bear the likeness of Jesus, the man from Heaven.*

Joni Eareckson Tada

My dear, sweet Allison,

The value of your beautiful smile, infectious laughter, and tender faith, challenged with a body crippled by cerebral palsy can never be measured in earthly terms. For twenty nine years you navigated an amazing journey at such a breathtaking pace, embracing a wide variety of earthly blessings and physically fragile challenges. And everyone you met along the way were always quick to become your next best friend. What a gift you were to so many. The fragrance of your life, your innocence, your acceptance of self, and consideration for others, enabled you to love well, in spite of your physical captivity, becoming a witness of God's supernatural love and compassionate grace. I don't ever remember you saying an unkind word about anyone. You are still changing lives since the day you were born. I promised you before you left this earth, kissing your wheelchair goodbye, this book would be written in your honor, and for God's glory. Your attitude was simply amazing. There were more than a dozen opportunities where you found yourself facing some pretty significant challenges: surgeries, installing rods, crushing and repacking your spine, removing parts of your colon, shots for muscle and joint pain, always with accompanying painful months of recovery. You could have easily caved in to your suffering and screamed about such an unfair journey, but you choose to fight instead, praying and believing for your very life, your friends lives, your hopes and your dreams - knowing full well how much you were loved, cared for and prayed for by so many. You knew where your true strength and hope came from, the Lord of *Heaven* and of earth, and that *Heaven's* reality would one day become sight. There was a defining moment on May 29th, 1985 at the age of eight after spending the evening out at our church's Awana program. Finally at home and sitting in your wheelchair waiting to be lifted into bed, that you made a decision to bow your head to pray a very humble and simple prayer asking Jesus to help you, forgive you, and come into your heart. With childlike faith, you wanted to make sure you were going to *Heaven*, and so you thanked Him for dying on the cross in your place, so you could have what He offers... *the gift of eternal life.*

At that exact moment your name was written in the Lambs book of life. It was explained to you that *Heaven* is a secure promise God gives to everyone who accepts Jesus in their hearts, and that you would never be snatched out of His loving hand.

"I give them eternal life, and no one can snatch them out of my hand."

John 10:28

"For God so loved the world that He gave His one and only Son, that whoever believes in him will not perish but have everlasting life."

John 3:16

These were the first two scriptures that you put your name into, inside your little Bible. "Whoever." You were the "whoever" at that precise moment, and without realizing it, this little prayer would change your life and your destiny forever. Jesus indeed answered that humble prayer as He promised to come in, and take up residence, to indwell your heart forever. It was then that He began to comfort you, assure you, and lead you by His love. He also gave you much needed courage by empowering your hope and growing your child like faith to enable you to put your trust in His love and His promises. He answered the cry of your own heart, to take your life and do something special with it, becoming the true 'Hero' in your own story. You learned that because of that prayer, your spirit was reborn. All because of Christ's love, as the true living bread that came down from *Heaven.*

> *[Appendix reference: 1 Corinthians 1, Isaiah 41:10*
> *Revelation 21:27, 2 Corinthians 5:17, John 6:51]*

I hope God will use this book to inspire parents of special needs children, and others who read it to recognize the living Hero in their own personal stories. Someone who promises to take up residence, making all things new as their personal savior, redeemer, provider, life coach, counselor, comforter, peacemaker, forever friend, blessed hope and divine physician. Someone who passionately waits to be unveiled and delights in making Himself known. He is not removed from our sufferings. He knows we are created in His likeness, and our lives here are preparing us for eternity. For as high as the *Heavens* are above the earth, His thoughts are higher, and He invites us to come prepare our hearts, to learn from Him, for the Kingdom of *Heaven* is not far from each of us.

> *[Appendix reference: 2 Corinthians 1:3*
> *Isaiah 9:6 John 14:2 Luke 5:20, Isaiah 55:1,*
> *Matthew 3:2, 4:17, Acts 17:24]*

Just as your birth was a beautiful mystery, a passage out of the physical womb into a world you had not yet imagined, so was your very last breath, releasing you to meet the person and the place you were destined for before the foundation of the world. Way beyond the scope of your earthly imagination. Those last few moments with you, cheek to cheek, were absolutely priceless. There are genuinely no human words to describe it or capture it. After visitors had stopped by to say their goodbyes, I just could not wait to sit down by your side, and simply take hold of your hand. I pondered once again the thousands of miles we had traveled together. Before I did however, I leaned over your peaceful face to whisper in your ear: "Ali, it's alright. Run home to *Heaven*, right into the loving arms of Jesus. Give Him the biggest kiss, and one day soon I will be running right behind."

What happened next I will never forget.

In a split-second, before I could even stand up straight, the pulse in your neck vanished. You left your frail body behind without one labored breath. Not one. There was such a supernatural peace in that room, I just stood and watched in amazement. I'm certain the room was full of activity I could not see, though I wish I could have. Angels were hovering around you – celebrating, laughing, and singing. They accompanied you safely home. A new home prepared with great detail, way beyond your wildest dreams just waiting, where God is dwelling with His creation, and where every tear was wiped away from your eyes. To the Kingdom of **Heaven**, where there is no more death, mourning, crying or pain, and where Jesus own radiance is a constant lamp.

I continued to stand motionless, with tears filling my eyes. I knew full well I was witnessing another miracle of God's amazing grace. His resurrection, life and power had reached down to take hold of your precious hand, gently taking away your breath only to receive you back unto Himself. God reached down from **Heaven** to do what only His amazing love, compassionate grace, and resurrection power can accomplish. He answered our 'on earth as it is **Heaven'** prayers. In those two seconds, you experienced the promise of the resurrection. And now you're absent from your earthly body, and present with the Lord.

[Appendix reference: Hebrews 1:14
John 14:1-3, Revelation 21: 1, 3-4]

That moment was so holy, so seamless, that not even a muscle in your physical body flinched. I am convinced, as close as we were, you were smiling and laughing already having tasted that liberating freedom awaiting you, along with your newly resurrected body, promised for **Heaven** where nothing ever breaks down, decays or corrupts... imperishable, free, and **totally** indestructible.

[Appendix reference: 2 Corinthians 5:8
1 Corinthians 15, 1 Peter 1:3]

That amazing moment has deepened my faith and transformed my sense of awe in Christ's Kingdom authority more than ever. Death is not only a shadow that could not *hold you,* nor can it *hold me.* As believers, we have an eternal inheritance in Christ that will never perish, spoil or fade. This world is not our final destination. Jesus is. *Heaven* is. He guarantees it, for He shed His blood for it. All you needed to do is have faith and believe that Jesus is the resurrection and the life, and the door. He knows it, that's why He told us straight up in His word: "I am the way, the truth, and the life. No one comes to the Father except through me." He is the bridge. He paid the price, and it really is all about Him securing the hope and anchoring forever, His promise of recovering our inheritance of everlasting life.

[Appendix reference: Psalm 23: 6, John 3:16
John 10:7 14:6, Hebrews 6: Hebrews 1:3
Isaiah 51:1 1 Peter 1:4, John 11:25, John 14:6]

I had witnessed once again, the maker of *Heaven* and earth at work. The God who created this glorious galaxy, stretching out its *Heavens*, and tucking the earth so perfectly within it, whose character can be tested and words eternally trusted.

Oh how I miss you Allison.

Until we meet again, when my own faith becomes sight,

Mother

02/ 13th/ 2007 by Jean Keaton

Chapter 2

Made in God's Image

For I know the plans I have for you, declares the LORD, plans to prosper you and not to harm you, plans to give you a hope and a future.

Jeremiah 29:11

Universally as parents, when expecting our first-born child, we are so elated and joyful over the anticipation of this amazing little miracle. With awe eyed wonder, after they are birthed into this world, we hear their first newborn cries, and watch in absolute astonishment their first coos and chuckles breaking into their first treasured smiles. Within that first year they go through such amazing development milestones.

They learn to roll, raise their heads, grasp toys, imitate sounds, recognize familiar faces, crawl, reach for objects, and work ever so hard in a million ways to pull themselves up to an upright stand, taking those first unsteady, courageous and wobbly first steps. We cheer them on, coaxing them, to take just a few more steps into our outstretched arms. We lift them high into the air and let them land, joy-filled, into our laps. Their expressions of joy and pride fill us with such contentment and purpose. But nothing compares to a parent's delight, when hearing for the very first time, they call out our name.

With the surprise of Allison's arriving two months prematurely in December of 1977, these expectations of my firstborn baby began to look so very different, as we headed into danger. My water broke, in the middle of the night, and I woke up startled to a soaking wet bed underneath me. I was taken by ambulance to Seattle's University Hospital to its neo-natal unit to deliver my premature baby. I was later told that either before or during her birth, the umbilical cord must have ended up wrapping around her tiny neck. Just as she joined the outside world, her newly formed brain was suddenly deprived of the precious oxygen it needed. For how long - from seconds to a few minutes - the doctors simply didn't know. But the diagnosis nine months later was certain: Cerebral Palsy. This meant brain damage affecting her entire physical body, as well as particular areas of her brain, and only time would tell as to what degree.

Soon after the wonderment and joy of receiving my firstborn baby girl came a tidal wave of pain. The diagnosis at nine months was so overwhelming, so devastating, I felt like I was being buried alive!! I couldn't breathe. I felt so inadequate, ill-equipped and helpless. And now, 33 years later as I am writing this, I can say with absolute assurance, our own personal narrative is filled with inspiration, confidence, courage and much hope. We began a race of faith, reaching out to the Creator of Heaven and of earth, who loves to make himself known and will tell you in His word, that before your were formed in your mother's womb, you were known, chosen, and set apart.

[Appendix reference: Jeremiah 1:5]

For the first five years after that frightening diagnosis I reached out in desperation to fix it, fix her, fix us, fix my marriage. I even wanted to fix other families' children I met when taking Allison to every conceivable medical treatment as well as therapies known to man. By the time Allison had reached her fifth birthday, two surgeries later and in a state of total exhaustion, I came to the end of my own resources. It became evidently clear she would never sit up or walk. She was already in a wheelchair, and her future - however long that would be - I was told would be filled with endless challenges. It was at this place of brokenness that I turned to the Bible, and discovered we were born into a much larger story. I started in the New Testament book of John, and read about a man born blind from birth. As I read and re-read this story, I discovered God's hand in his birth, his purpose, God's plan, God's glory, and the amazing hope and eternal promise of *Heaven.* My own blind eyes were opened to see we were created by Him and for Him with a glory all our own. Each one of us are His own workmanship created for a specific purpose ordained from before the foundation of the world. I may not understand it all, but a healing balm began to soothe my tired and worn out exhausted soul. This new found faith birthed within me a sustaining hope, and authentic transformation of heart. He began to meet our needs, where we needed it most. And as I discovered over time, all things are possible with faith, hope, love and diligence.

Allison's Cerebral Palsy had left her in a physically fragile condition, affecting her entire body except her speech (she started speaking at the age of three). She was diagnosed as quadriplegic and epileptic. In our case, it meant that she would never walk, never have full motor control over her hands, and she would suffer from seizures her whole life. For the entire duration of her twenty-nine years, she was completely dependent on others for her basic needs. Her mother, brother, step-father, extended family, and friends put in tens of thousands of hours to care for her physical needs, and ensure her medication. Her father and step-mother, both nurses, provided nonstop medical wisdom, emotional support, and physical care. Our extended "medical family" – the community of doctors, nurses, and aides that we grew to know and love – also provided a tremendous amount of support. It took a team to raise Allison. By God's grace, I was able to lift her, carry her, bath her, feed her, cloth her, and love her every day. From wheelchair to wheelchair, our lives together were filled with all the joy and toil you can find this side of Heaven.

Other than a very beautiful willing heart, and an inquiring intelligent mind, she was powerless to contribute to her physical needs. Her life was spent at the humble end of requests for personal care. Up unto her very last breath, she totally trusted, that out of love, her care needs would be met.

Yet still – there was nothing on this earth that could have sustained her spirit for twenty-nine years. It was only the love of God that roused her heart to battle every morning. The divine love that she received was in turn reflected back to those around her. To us – her friends and family. That love - the love that sustained her - is waiting for all of us.

Chapter 3

Kissing Her
Wheelchair Goodbye

O n February 13th 2007 at 2:00 o'clock in the after-
noon, Allison kissed this earth, her loved ones and
her wheelchair a final goodbye. I was now staring down
at her fragile body where I could clearly see the color fade
quickly from her peaceful face, leaving her frail body now
empty, no longer inhabiting her living soul. Her spirit
was gone. She left this earth in all its beauty and struggle
to a more glorious country, a *Heavenly* one, full of resurrection hope, promise, love, and the unending promise
of living in God's presence forever. I was witnessing the
truth of what we had celebrated, read about, cried about,
even danced about, and especially sang songs about
so many times together, that death was only a passing

shadow, smoke and mirrors. *Heaven's* promises are truly our celebrated hope and anticipated future.

[Appendix reference: Hebrews 11:16, Psalm 23:4]

She was now *more alive* than ever, having received the goal of her faith. A supernatural joyous *inheritance* that will never get old or ever again, wear itself out. Ali had looked to the rock, from which she was cut, Jesus the image of the invisible God, now exalted and sitting down at the right hand of the Father in *Heaven*, the creator of *Heaven* and of earth.

[Appendix reference: 2 Corinthians5:8, 1 Peter 1:4,
Isaiah 51:1, Hebrews 12:2]

Allison did not end, she was expectant and hopeful of a brand new life. A far different reality with a resurrected body... created just for her, waiting and promised through God's breathed word, where all things will be made new, with a well detailed home designed just for her as a citizen of *Heaven*. She is now home, where she will see the author and perfecter of her faith, who created her for love, and eternal fellowship.

[Appendix reference: 2 Timothy 3:16 Isaiah 25:8,
Revelation 21:4, Revelation 5:5, Hebrews 12:2]

Throughout her life, she loved music. In particular worship music. Singing and making melody with her voice, not to mention hiding every single word down inside her heart. Her recall was quite amazing. What a precious heritage of belief. It's actually God's prescription for growth, through the memorizing of His word, all the while transforming, empowering, and training her (us) to walk by faith in His integrity, and not by sight.

[Appendix reference: Romans 12:1,
Luke 23:43, 2 Corinthians 5:7]

So Allison relocated, as she breathed her very last breath to where I can no longer see her from here. For the first time she flew out of her crippled body that never allowed her to take her first steps, brush her own hair, or write her own name without struggle. To that glorious and exciting Kingdom shared with millions of other believers, and the worshipping class of angels. A Kingdom without shadows, tears, suffering, shame, fear, rejection, sin or death in any form. And Christ alone is its lamp. Her leaving wasn't an end. It was only an interruption before joining another world, - wonderful beyond imagination!

I had loved her, cherished her, and carried her, as far as I could this side of *Heaven*, with a multitude of caring people that added so much joy and value to her life. I am convinced Allison was escorted by angels who were singing with her, dancing with her, praising God with her. She was escorted right to *Heaven's* gates, to meet the person and the place she was created for. Jesus Christ, "*Heaven's* Lamb of God" who said with signs and wonders following:

[Appendix reference: Revelation 7:7, 21:22, John 11:25]

"I am the resurrection and the life. He who believes in me will live, even though he dies; and whoever lives and believes in me will never die.
Do you believe this?"

John 11:25-26

Ask, seek, and knock and the door will be opened
Revelation 21:23

This one thing I know, if she could interrupt the worship, she would testify from her heart as loudly as her' new set of lungs could sing, one of her favorite songs that she loved and sang repeatedly titled: "Testify to Love" by Avalon:

All the colors of the rainbow
All the voices of the wind
Every dream that reaches out
That reaches out to find where love begins
Every word of every story,
Every star in every sky
Every corner of creation lives to testify
For as long as I shall live
I will testify to love
I'll be a witness in the silences when words are not enough
With every breath I take I will give thanks to God above
For as long as I shall live
I will testify to love
From the mountains to the valleys,
From the rivers to the sea
Every hand that reaches out
Every hand that reaches out to offer peace
Every simple act of mercy
Every step to Kingdom come

All the Hope in every heart
Will speak what love has done.

We both discovered that God is a covenant keeping God, with the sign of a "rainbow" sealing His promise. He tells us in His word that we will also find a rainbow in *Heaven* resembling an emerald encircling His very throne. *I can imagine Allison's excitement by it's brilliance - giggling with sheer delight!*

[Appendix reference: Genesis 9:13, Revelation 4:3]

Miss Allison Kristine Hahnel

12/15/77 – 02/13/2007

Chapter 4

Before You Were Born

One day soon my own lease will be up on this earth, and then it will be Allison's turn to greet me with a kiss, and I will get to witness with my own eyes, her resurrected body functioning wholly at unimaginable speeds. And we will rejoice together singing another one of her favorite songs:

I have a Maker,
He formed my heart,
Before even time began,
My life was in His hands.
He knows my name,
He knows my every thought,
He sees each tear that falls,
And hears me when I call

I have a Father,

He calls me His own,

He'll never leave me,

No matter where I will go,

He knows my name

He knows my every thought

He sees each tear that fell,... and hears me when I call.

By Tommy Walker 1996

The Bible tells us clearly that the same God who created the *Heavens* and laid the foundations of the earth, calling each star by its own name, with not one of them missing, has also created you for a divine purpose, a divine plan, and He knows your name. In fact, even before the foundations of the earth, He ordained your very birth, and He knows you intimately.

[Appendix Reference: Isaiah 51: 13, Psalm 147:4

Isaiah 40:26, Isaiah 24: 24, Psalm 139: 2]

Let's start with the wonder of your very own birth. You can read about your own created heartbeat in the one hundred and thirty-ninth psalm. If you don't yet own a Bible, find one, ask for one, or go to our website, and I will make sure to send you one. I will never forget the first time I laid my own eyes on its truth some twenty eight years ago at the age of thirty two. It became a living waterfall that washed over my grief stricken soul from the top of my head to the very soles of my feet, and it began a walk of grace and liberation through every need, circumstance, heartache and care.

I believed that Jesus died for my sins, and that He created me because He loved me. It wasn't complicated... I just humbled my heart, and I asked him to come in, forgive me of all my sins, past, present and future, and give me the assurance of everlasting life I was so hungry for. I was 'born again' with *Heaven* as my new hope and future destination. Jesus moved in to become my very own personal Savior, and forever friend. Like a butterfly emerging out of its cocoon, God's word was a liberating love letter written just to me. For the first time I understood that God loves me with an everlasting love, and He created me for fellowship. To be part of His family.

The Scriptures say that He rewards those who diligently seek Him through the study of His word and simple conversational prayer. Telling Him everything and learning to cast it on Him. Not to try and fix it. A real transformation begins, supernaturally by the power of His Spirit, and you become a partaker of God's divine nature.

[Appendix reference: Isaiah 40:22, 26, Romans 12:2 1 John 4:8, Romans 12:1, 1 Peter 1:4, Colossians 2:7]

God's Spirit and Word unveil the mystery and sig-
nificance of your very own fingerprint. He will open your
eyes to see that you are made in God's very image, and
His likeness. Psalm 139:13, is God breathed, stating that
without a doubt you are both fearfully and wonderfully
created, as He knit you together in your mother's womb,
for a divine purpose and divine destiny. While you were
still in your mother's womb, all the days ordained for your
life, were written before even one of them came into being.
Think of it. What profound purpose and meaning to your
existence. Even before the foundation of the world, God
had planned your very birth, and your adoption through
Christ into His family... as well as good works that He
prepared in advance for each and every one of us to do.
Don't move too fast. Let that sink in deeply.

[Appendix reference: Ephesians 1: 5,

Ephesians 2:10, Romans 8: 23]

He very skillfully endowed you with gifts — the
seeds of great promise and great potential. He separated
you and appointed you for a specific glory all your own.
You truly are His workmanship, born for this time in his-
tory to bring forth fruits, uniquely all your own, that no
one but you can fulfill. And He has loved you with His

41

eternal love. God is Love, and you are priceless and irreplaceable to him.

[Appendix reference: Psalm 139: 15, 16,
Eph 2:10, Jeremiah 31:3]

Leaving no details to chance, He knows the number
of your days, when you rise and when you lie down. He
knows the color of your eyes, the inflections of your voice,
and the uniqueness of your DNA and fingerprint. Even
the very hairs on your head are numbered. Astounding!
It's all recorded right in God's word. God sees your abundant potential hidden even to yourself that he wants to
unveil. He wants to empower, strengthen, guide, train,
teach, correct, equip, transform, celebrate, and yes even
reward you, by the power of his Spirit.

[Appendix reference: Genesis 1:26, Psalm 139: 16,
Luke 12:7, Matt 10:30, Rev 22: 12]

He is *crazy in love* with you, and just in case you
did not know, intimately acquainted with all your ways.
Nothing in your life is arbitrary. Your eternal Creator
left no details to chance. Even in this fallen world, when
life at times doesn't make sense, God always has a plan
for you, and He specializes in knowing how to work all
things together for good. To give you a future and a hope.

And it is hidden in Christ both in **Heaven** and on earth. He designed each of us for a specific purpose, a specific work, as we are made into Christ likeness.

> *[Appendix reference: Psalm 139: 3-4, Romans 8:28*
> *Jeremiah 29:11 Colossians 1:10, 3:2-4]*

Although your circumstances might seem to you totally unfair, and you have shed many tears I well understand, because so far your life has not gone exactly as you have dreamed, and at times it may all seem all together pointless. God can turn it all around by His Spirit. There is still a dream to be lived out, a dream to be fulfilled, knit deeply down inside you. You can't deny it or even begin to fulfill it on your own. There is something missing if you are yet without Christ as your personal Savior and you can feel it. There will be a longing in your heart you can't put your finger on, a big hole, an emptiness that you can't possibly fill. No one can. Even though you may travel the entire world searching.

> *[Appendix reference: Psalm 139: 5,*
> *John 15:16, 1 Peter 1:18]*

God is a Father. A loving **Heavenly** Father who created you on purpose so He can love you, fill you with His Spirit. And He longs for that love in return. In fact, remember He rewards those who hunger and seek to know Him, please Him because He loves to be found. He is not far from each one of our hearts. He treasures relationships and wants a family, and He created you to be a part of it. The Bible calls it 'the good news.' And that is what the pages of this book are all wrapped around. God is the God of the invitations and He gives us the free will to look into His face and learn the secrets of eternity. Once that desire is sparked within and we open up our hearts, He promises to make himself known.

> *[Appendix reference: Jeremiah 31: 3, Mark 1:14,*
> *Isaiah 55:1, 6 Revelation 3:20, Hebrews 11:6]*

"You will find me," God says, "when you seek me with all of your heart."

> *Jeremiah 29: 13*

What an amazing privilege that we may choose to love Him and live.

Chapter 5

What Went Wrong

It's important for all of us to understand this story we've been born into, going all the way back to the Garden of Eden found in the beginning of Genesis. Just like you and I, Adam and Eve (our first parents) were created to bear God's likeness and nature and to fellowship and enjoy Him forever. He had surrounded them with every conceivable blessing and gave them a home to take care, to steward, like no other. God saw everything that He had created and saw that it was good. Very good. And then He rested with His creation.

[Appendix reference: Genesis 1:26, 28
Genesis 2:3 Genesis 3:15]

They had their boundaries clearly set for their provision of abundance, divinely designed to multiply and expand the Garden of Eden while living and enjoying complete fellowship with God as their Father, and each other. In the middle of the garden where He had placed them were the tree of life, and the tree of the knowledge of good and evil. God's original plan for Adam and Eve did not include shame, guilt, suffering, sin or death. They were surrounded by God's affirming love and covering presence. He had provided for an abundant multiplied life, of power, and dominion under His loving and wise authority, asking that they only refrain from eating from the tree of the knowledge of good and evil. They were capable of not sinning by their own voluntary wills through obedience. The book of Romans speaks of Adam's "transgression," as meaning He stepped over the line, which was clearly laid out and protected by God's goodness and grace..

[Appendix reference: Genesis 2:8
Genesis 2: 15 -17 Romans 5:14]

Sadly, however, Adam and Eve fell prey to Satan's seduction of questioning God's goodness, tempting them to disobey God's known will, His one and only restriction, by desiring to eat from the tree of the knowledge of good and evil, taking that which did not belong to them. This act of treason, for that is what it was, ushered in the towering consequences of sin and death, and they ran away from this violation of conscience... to hide. Not just a physical death... back to dust... but also a spiritual death as well.

[Appendix reference: Genesis 2:7]

Through this open act of rebellion, Adam and Eve found themselves kicked out of the Garden of Eden, and then removed from God's protective covering presence. They were now declared unholy, in their fallen condition breaking their fellowship with God, leaving a breach so wide that all of creation was affected. The Father's just love had clearly warned them, and He is bound by His own word. Adam and Eve with their own free wills, had given their freedom away, as well as their fellowship, betrayed through their choice. So their relationship and likeness was crippled, and their protected paradise was lost. A new battle for the human heart was now at stake. So God came up with His plan to restore mankind back to His original state. They were captive and now lost in their present condition, still created in the image of God, but now paralyzed and hostage through this new fallen nature to sin. Totally powerless within themselves to change it, God knows that they cannot function properly without His presence, His covering, so He gets directly involved to do whatever is necessary to redeem them back. To restore them completely back to their original eternal state, and not let them die separated from their creator.

[Appendix reference: Genesis 3:1-24]

If Adam and Eve had continued to live in the garden eating from the tree of life, they would have lived forever enjoying God's protection and abiding presence. No curse of sin or death. But now, their fallen state would mean forever separated, So God declared His plan to go after his creation, to seek, save, and rescue that which was lost. Through one act of love, death on a cross, this curse would be forever reversed, and fellowship with God restored. The human race was now captive in the worst possible way. In its fallen state the human heart will always lead itself astray totally powerless within itself to fix this fallen condition... now darkened in understanding, as if seeing through a glass darkly.

[Appendix reference: Romans 5:6, Romans 8:3,
Ephesians 4:17-19, 1 Corinthians 13:12]

"But God's proof of love" trumps their (and our) confusion, blame, and shame, for he searches them out where they were hiding, by calling out their names. To let them know He has always wanted their love, their fellowship, and He provides special clothing (provision) for them, and it came in the 'gift' of His Son.

[Appendix reference: Genesis 3:15, John 3:16]

You can now locate the fall of our first set of parents. The consequence of sin and death was passed along to the entire human race. The 'seed of the woman' is Jesus God's son, who later came down from *Heaven* to win back that which was lost *(our citizenship and our inheritance)*... as the ransom payment for our sin against a holy God. He died on a cross that you may live, as a born-again legal heir to the throne.

[Appendix reference: Ephesians 2:12 Galatians 4:7]

One favorite story that paints this so beautifully can be found threaded through the book of second Samuel, right after the book of Ruth in the Old Testament. It is wrapped around a five year old boy named Mephibosheth. He was a prince, an heir to the throne as the first grandson to King Saul, the first King of Israel. News hit the royal palace one day, that both His father Jonathan and His Grandfather King Saul were killed together in battle. Mephibosheph's nurse, knowing that little Mephibosheph might be the next to die, since he was a royal heir and a very real threat to the throne... grabbed him into her arms and ran from the palace for their very lives. While she was frantically running she dropped Him, and He became crippled in both feet from the fall. Because His life was in real danger, his nurse carried him all the way as they fled to Lo Debar, where they were far enough away to hide. Now many years had passed, and Mephibosheth had to learn how to live as an orphan, cut off from his inheritance, and everything that was rightfully his to enjoy. Years later, when King David Israel's second king had settled his own affairs and subdued his enemies, he remembered the covenant he had made with Saul's son Jonathon (Mephibosheth's father) long before ever becoming King. He promised Prince Jonathan based on their sincere love for one another, that He would always show kindness to his household, never allowing his household to be cut off from his inherited blessings.

[Appendix reference: 2 Samuel 4:4 1
Samuel 20:13-15, 2 Samuel 9:1]

David did not know about Mephbiosheth, but one day he inquired about the whereabouts of any of Jonathan's relatives. And one of Saul's servants still serving at the palace remembered Mephibosheth, knowing exactly where he could be found. King David requested he be brought to the palace right away. So David's soldiers went to find him, and in fear and trembling Mephibosheth was brought back to the palace once again, certain he would not live to see another day. When He arrived and was brought before the King, he bowed in his presence falling with his face to the floor. Seeing that he was fearful King David said, "don't be afraid... for I will surely show you kindness for the sake of your father Jonathan. I will restore to you all the land that belonged to your Grandfather Saul by a royal decree, and you will always eat at my table." And Mephbiosheth lived in Jerusalem, completely restored, and was treated as one of King David's sons, eating at His table forever. He was also given many servants to help him till and harvest the land he received as his rightful inheritance.

This is another beautiful portrait that pictures the unconditional love of God that reaches across all barriers to restore and reconcile us back to Himself. The relationship between King David and Mephibosheth is meant to show us the grace filled merciful way God reaches out to find us, treating us as heirs, with no strings attached. As a fallen race, crippled by the fall, we had lost everything, and were under the sentence of sin and death, but in Christ we have regained our status of son ship through adoption, being fully restored into the family of God, with full rights as citizens in *Heaven*... and we are invited to eat with Him at His table forever.

[Appendix reference: 2 Samuel 9:7 Revelation 3:20]

"Blessed be the God and Father of our Lord Jesus Christ, who has blessed us with every spiritual blessing in the *Heavenly* places in Christ, just as He chose us in Him before the foundation of the world, that we should be holy and blameless before Him. In love, He predestined us to adoption as sons through Jesus Christ to Himself, according to the kind intention of His will, to the praise of the glory of His grace, which He freely bestowed on us in the beloved."

[Appendix reference: Ephesians 1:3-6]

Now if we are children (believers), then we are heirs—heirs of God and co-heirs with Christ.

[Appendix reference: Romans 8:17]

If you belong to Christ, then you are Abraham's seed, and heirs according to the promise.

[Appendix reference: Galatians 3:29]

He (Our *Heavenly* Father) might show the incomparable riches of His grace, expressed in His kindness to us in Jesus Christ.

[Appendix reference: Ephesians 2:7]

David said to him, "For I will surely show you kindness for the sake of your father Jonathan. I will restore to you all the land that belonged to your grandfather Saul and you will always eat at my table."

[Appendix reference: 2 Samuel 9:7]

Chapter 6

Jesus Got It Back

❦

Jesus secured our inheritance that will never perish, spoil or die.

As I did for Allison what she was powerless to do for herself, Jesus stepped in to do for us, what we were powerless to do for ourselves. Jesus willingly came down from *Heaven* to die a crucified death on that cross that through His death, burial, and resurrection He won back an inheritance for us that can never perish, spoil or fade- kept in Heaven securing forever our fellowship with the Father, our adoption and our citizenship in *Heaven*. He now holds the *keys* over sin and death.

[Appendix reference: John10:11, 18
Philippians' 3:20,1Peter 1:3, 2 Peter 1:4]

In Allison's vulnerable and physically paralyzed condition, she needed 'hands on intervention'... total care from another human being to keep her alive, safe and protected. She was absolutely powerless to care for herself, powerless to protect herself, and for twenty nine years remained totally dependent on others to meet all of her physical needs. From carrying, bathing, dressing, transferring, feeding, to navigating her wheelchair, and most importantly, to loving. Left to herself she would die. I did for her what she was unable to do for herself. Costly? Absolutely. But driven by a million steps of love that taught me along its journey, to lay down my life for her care.

[Appendix reference: Ephesians 2:1, 8, 12, 13]

Jesus, knowing his destiny, left his surroundings in *Heaven* and came down to earth to rescue us from our fallen sinful state. Left to ourselves we would die, eternally separated from the Father, and still captive in our sin, powerless to fix it.. He lovingly pursues us to look to Him, with desire. A desire to want to know Him, recognizing His voice through His written word, distinct from all others. *Amazing love.* Jesus *chose...* to die that you may live. He laid down His life as the spotless lamb of God, that you may be rescued and pardoned, so you could once again live forever in God's Holy presence, becoming a partaker of God's divine nature escaping the corruption of this world caused by evil desires. Costly? Beyond our comprehension. He was driven by love to liberate us, and set us free forever from the power of sin and death. The only way out was the cross.

Heaven's door has one *Key*, and *Jesus now holds it.*

From eternity past, if it had only been you, Jesus would have willingly come down from *Heaven* to die in your place, so that you may have eternal life. This is the kindness of God our Savior and His love that rescues the powerless. This is the story you have been born into. Belief in Christ restores us back into fellowship. That was God's plan since the fall in the garden. He always has a plan. Because He first created you to love you, He invites you to draw near... that you can enjoy His faithful lasting love and fellowship forever.

[Appendix reference: Titus 3:4-8]

No longer alienated from God, Jesus reconciled you by His own body through death, in order to present you holy in God's sight without blemish as Heirs... free from accusation. Oh what crazy marvelous grace. Jesus is the" Hero" that stepped in to rescue us from the law of sin and death. That He could indwell us, and one day takes us home to Heaven. Oh what a Loving Living and Marvelous Savior.

[Appendix reference: Romans 6:10
Hebrew 1:10, Colossians 1:22 Romans 8:1]

You cannot earn it, fix it, work for it, and you surely don't deserve it. Salvation is a free gift of God's amazing grace. To anyone who will believes with childlike faith. Whoever... whenever... wherever. You can't clean yourself up, so quit trying. He is waiting. And He will take you just as you are...sitting, running, walking, crawling, or riding in your wheelchair. With sight, or without it, in deafness or in hearing. The greatest gift we can receive this side of *Heaven* is to be restored back into a right relationship with our *Heavenly* Creator. If you don't yet know him, this is what your searching for, longing for...what you have been missing. Do you know Him as your Heavenly Father, with Christ as your personal Savior? I pray you simply bow your head wherever you are, and ask Jesus to come into your heart, to forgive you of your sins, so that you can become a new creation in Christ. And He will come in with His Divine Nature to put your heart at rest so you can eat at His table and *dine with Him forever.*

[Appendix reference: Ephesians 2:8, Romans 6:10,
2 Corinthians 5:17, 2 Peter 1:4]

If you just took that step of faith and prayed to receive Christ into your heart, welcome to the Family of God. The Bible says your name has been recorded into the Lambs book of life. And that the angels in *Heaven* are rejoicing every time someone comes to Christ. It's a mystery that you can now wrap your heart around.

[Appendix reference: Ephesians 1:9]

Behold I stand at the door and knock. If anyone hears my voice and opens the door, I will come in and eat with him, and he with me.

[Appendix reference: Revelation 3:20, Revelation 21:27]

Chapter 7

Words Of Comfort

Do not let your hearts be troubled. Trust in God, trust also in me. In my Father's house are many rooms; if it were not so, I would have told you. I am going there to prepare a place for you. And if I go and prepare a place for you, I will come back and take you to be with me that you also may be where I am.

John 14: 1-3

Jesus who has mirrored the forgiving power and satisfying love of our *Heavenly* Father is now only hours away from laying down his own life crucified on a cross. His disciples still didn't understand the enormous battle awaiting him. How He would lay down His life as the spotless lamb – the perfect sacrifice — to pay for the sins of the entire world. Amazingly you can find Jesus reminding, comforting, and reassuring his disciples of their *inheritance* that is coming both on earth, and in *Heaven* through their union with Him. He knows he will be leaving them soon, securing forever their eternal destination. To help them understand the magnitude of this separation, He reminds them of a Jewish wedding. They would well understand its covenant promise... for the betrothed husband goes on ahead to prepare a place of great value for his bride, while she waits in great anticipation for His return. He will prepare the way, the place, and their home together, coming back for her soon so they can be together always. And she remains waiting in faith with eager expectation for their future together as husband and wife in a covenant union with their own dwelling place.

He will come take us to a place so lavish, so extravagant, so prepared, there is no need of a sun, moon, or stars to shine upon it. The Glory of God lightens it, and its lamp will be our redeemer and friend. God has exalted Him as our forerunner. All of *Heaven* is His throne with the constant radiance of emerald encircling it. From there He will rule over everything else.

He is not content to dwell there without His people. He is not content to live there without you. So while you are still here, open up your Bible, Gods love letter to you, and make *Heaven* your own personal study. You will be thrilled at how much He reveals and how He loves to reward your heart. There is no greater quest, than to get to know God through His eternal word. His word is settled in *Heaven*, with thousands of believers that have gone on before us!

[Appendix reference: Revelation 4:3]

Is your heart expectant and fully assured that *Heaven* is your final destination, that Jesus will come to take you where He is, and that He has promised you a place that He Himself has prepared with great detail just for you? That He created you because He loves you, to give you a future and a hope? Allison understood when she asked Jesus to came into her heart, He would come in to dwell forever, never letting go of her hand, giving her His strength, His love, and His power to live on earth for His Glory. She saw to what great lengths He would go to send her loving assurance and comfort... even up to her very last breath where she departed in a twinkling of an eye, leaving with great joy, to be joining God's family in *Heaven*, where she (and you) will never have to say good bye again.

This is the story you have been born into, that God is working out through Jesus, his Son, who came *to pardon you from all your sins, to redeem you, and restore you to*

61

Himself, to relationship, and to live in *Heaven* where His story and yours will continue to be written.

What was lost, Jesus got back! The gift of eternal life, an *inheritance* that will never perish, spoil or fade—kept in *Heaven* for you! He hold the keys to the Kingdom! As believers, you and I have this blessed assurance. *Our inheritance is in Christ, and we will gather at our Father's table forever!*

> *"And If I go and prepare a place for you,*
> *I will come back and take you to be with me*
> *that you also may be where I am."*
> *John 14:3*

Amazing Grace

*Amazing Grace, how sweet the sound, that saved a
wretch like me.*
*I once was lost, but now am found, was blind, but
now I see.*

*Twas Grace that taught my heart to fear. And Grace,
my fears relieved.*
*How precious did that Grace appear, the hour I first
believed.*

*Through many dangers, toils and snares I have
already come;*
*Tis Grace that brought me safe thus far and Grace
will lead me home.*

*The Lord has promised good to me. His word my hope
secures.*
*He will my shield and portion be, As long as life
endures.*

*Yea, when this flesh and heart shall fail,
And mortal life shall cease, I shall possess within the
veil,*

A life of joy and peace.
When we've been here ten thousand years bright
shining as the sun.

We've no less days to sing God's praise
Then when we've first begun.

Amazing Grace, how sweet the sound,
That saved a wretch like me.

I once was lost and now am found,
Was blind, but now I see.

By John Newton (1725-1807)

Chapter 8

A few precious memories of Allison

Following are memories of my daughter as shared by her many friends.

My Niece, My Mentor!

Relationships are a gift of God and meant to be nurtured. I can honestly say that I learned this from the women in my family who have given great gifts of time and energy in the support of their children. My sister, Meredith and my niece Allison, are my greatest examples. Meredith poured into Allison's life unconditional love and joy that 'spilled out' all over anyone within her circle of influence…and I am sure beyond what we can see. Allison was defined by her spirit, her courage, and her forgiveness! A great interest in others marked Allison's personality. She loved surprises, loved to be teased (by Uncle Darrel), and loved to be with you. Always quick with a question: "What's new in your life?" and "How are you?" not wanting to waste a precious second of interaction! Her engaging smile drew people close and there wasn't a person involved with Ali that wasn't a NEW friend. She knew how to hold her friendships loosely in order to keep them. This "catch n release" approach allowed Allison to delight in those around her and appreciate the moment at hand. Allison's sweetness and appreciative heart never seemed to be daunted by the limiting circumstances of her Cerebral Palsy. In spite of difficulties, challenges, and limitations Allison rose above without complaint or a broken spirit. Her Lion-sized Heart of courage was evident – she was a fighter! Her discernment knew what was important and of lasting value and helped her accept the things she couldn't change. Her bravery and trust allowed her to ask the hard questions: "When am I going to walk?", and later "Am I going to die?" She trusted in her parents and their loving support; and she trusted in the Lord and His plan for her life. What a wonderful gift to be forgiven – of anything. You could go any amount of time without seeing Ali and she wouldn't even bring it up – her joy just to be with you would be evident! I never knew of anyone Ali held bad feelings for…even God. If she pondered: "Why me?" any bitterness that could have changed her spirit never stuck! Ali knew how precious life is and how to love keeping no record of wrongs! How I miss my sweet niece and her gift for laughter and fun. Always we would leave our time together with a new perspective and appreciation for life! Now, Ali has gone ahead and one last message for her family and friends rings forth.

From her Spirit: "I am so excited to know you, and thankful you're in my life!" I love you guys!"

From her Courage: "Don't be afraid," "Be strong and courageous – don't lean on your own understanding – trust God in all his ways!" "In this world you will have trouble but God has overcome it!"

From her Forgiven Heart: "There is nothing you have done that is too awful or too big for God to handle. Ask Him. Seek Him with all your heart...and I can't wait to see you again!"

From her New Home: "God has changed my sorrow into dancing, removed my infirmity and clothed me with joy, that my heart may sing to you and not be silent...O Lord my God, I give you thanks forever!" (Psalm 30:11)

Aunt Cici Hume

I will always remember Allison as she wheeled into our worship center. I always tried to greet her which was usually met with a big smile and a warm hug. She was always a person on the go and I remember when the FWM wheelchairs started — wow it was so exciting to do and think about all the possibilities. Strange as it may be my fondest memory was preaching at Allison's memorial service. She had lived a life so well but as I looked into the audience that day there were many of her friends in their wheelchairs. I was overwhelmed with thoughts of our Jesus — how on the cross he was nailed down and couldn't move the way He wanted to — I spoke directly to those in their wheelchairs about how much Jesus understood their frustrations with being confined because He was restricted on the cross. As I wept I went and touched each one of them and blessed them. Truly our hope and glory to God is that there will be "NO Wheelchairs In Heaven."

Steve Scroggins

Pastor

North County Christ the King Church

Allison had a great zest for life. The sharing of stories about her friends and especially the boy friends' always made her smile, laughing together. She loved her family and wanted to be kept up to date about what was going on especially about cousin Will. Ali was in Liza's wedding as a bridesmaid. She was beautiful and took the family responsibility with pride. Being the older sister is another responsibility she took seriously and Brandon was often put in his place by Ali's sharp wit. Her personality and thoughtfulness concerning other people made Ali very special. I will tell you she was a trooper through the years. Even though she was physically confined to a wheelchair Ali was mentally and emotionally involved outside herself. Ali, we love you and miss you very much.

Uncle Laury and Aunt Mary Evans

Oh my sweet friend Allison. You were such a wonderful light in this world. With all your suffering you were still able to bring such joy and laughter to the rest of us. I have many great memories of times shared with you. It warms my heart to know that you are with our Heavenly Father and there is no more pain for you. Just your beautiful smile. I can hardly wait to be together again. Thank you for all that you are, and all that you shared. Always your friend, Gail.

Gail Parker

The day I met Allison I was training to be a receptionist at the care center where she was living. As the glass doors opened Allison wheeled through them and came up to the front desk introducing herself, and shared that she was getting ready for a public speaking engagement. WOW I was blown away and very impressed. That was the first day of a beautiful friendship. We later that month moved into a brand new care center where I would see her and we would head down to the ice cream store down the street with my daughter (who was 8 years old at the time) and we had such fun together. We would play games in the conference center where she lived and we would invite other to play as well. Allison was always concerned about others and their well being. She would pray for the NAC's that took care of her and the nurses. And as much pain as Allison was in, she seemed always more concerned for others. One being her father. She would ask me in a daily basis to please pray for him and that he would find a personal relationship with God. I would get off my evening shift at 9:00 pm and go to her room that was just right around the corner...and she would always hear me before I could even announce myself or knock, and she would say: "Shelly come on in and see me, I can hear you." I too have Cerebral Palsy and I think she could hear my canes I use to walk with. So I would go in and she was all ready for bed laying there like an angel and we would talk a bit, and share, watch our favorite tv program, or read together before I would head on home. There is a song that is played on the radio often called "Testify To Love" and that was

Allison's song and it will always be her song. I hear it in the car and at times have to pull over because the tears still come. My daughter will say, "hey mom…they are playing Allison's song."

Shelley Mangum Simpson

Meredith and Allison had such a unique bond together as mother and daughter, inseparable they were. I knew Allison ever since the day she was born. Ali endured many hardships throughout her life. A lot of pain, medications, not to mention numerous operations. Every time a new obstacle would come her way, I would get a call from Meredith. We would always petition the throne room on Allison's behalf…, that God's Grace would get her through this next challenge, and comfort Her as only He can do with his power and strength. It just amazes me to see how the good Lord was always with Allison through everything. He would always pick out the best care givers, the best friends, and Ali had quite a few. I never really looked at Allison with her disability, but as a person first. Much of her life was so full of joy. Despite her disabilities she had a pretty normal and active life as other children do thanks to a loving mother who devoted herself to her daughter. They both knew God's Grace would prove sufficient. Its only His Love that would see them through.

I can do all things through Christ who strengthens me. (Philippians 4:13)

Casting all your cares on the Lord, for He cares for you. (1 Peter 5:7)

We miss you Allison but I know we will see you in Heaven leaping and jumping... doing all those things you couldn't do here on this earth. That will bring us such happiness and joy.

Sharon Jordan

Allison, so many wonderful thoughts come to my mind when I think and remember "Ali". Allison was an amazing young lady that touched so many people. Here was a young woman dependent on others for pretty much everything, but in the next breath she was fiercely independent. Even though she lived her life in a wheelchair, she certainly did not let it become an obstacle to leading a very busy life. At times busier than an able bodied person like myself. Whether it was working at the ARC, or passionately speaking on the rights of the disabled, or just hanging out with her family and friends, Allison did all that and more in her short life. One thing that really made a huge impression on me was that Ali seldom if rarely complained about her health. Here she was full speed at times as if she was on a mission. More energy than I had myself at times. Allison also had an infectious smile, that no matter what your day may have been like, she would smile and laugh and you couldn't help but to join in. Ali also loved to watch old TV shows like the Golden Girls or a good Hallmark movie. Along with that she would have her friends come to sit at her bedside and join in on the fun. She also shared her Love of the Lord and how truly blessed she was. She was blessed with loving parents and especially an unbelievable mother. While Allison was not physically able to walk, it was her mom who did that and so much more for 'miss Ali'. But most of all it was her mother who raised a God loving and compassionate young lady. Even though Ali is no longer with us now, I know she is free and healthy in Heaven. No more wheelchair, seizures or pain. Free to run, and laugh, and make more friends.. Free in the arms of her Precious Lord and Savior.

Allison, many a day I have missed you and thought to myself. "What would Ali say"?

But Ali, wait patiently for me, as one day we will be together again in Heaven and what a reunion we will have on that day. "Love and Hugs Ali"...

Grace Assink

I remember how many lives were touched in third world countries when Allison and her mom worked on raising funds to purchase wheelchairs. I fondly remember one evening on March 31st 2006, at our church Ladies Spa Night. The big event of the night after all the pampering was: "For the ultimate cleansing—get Baptized." Well I remember Allison was set on being baptized that evening. Although during that portion of the night...waiting for perhaps more than a dozen or so women getting fully immersed in the baptismal tank, Allison began to fall asleep. Her mother thought it best to wait until another time, to which Allison woke and said NO. Let's do it now. So we did and the smile on her face was unforgettable. I will not forget that moment.

Jolynn Gilliam
Director of Womens' Ministry
North County Christ the King

Allison had a significant influence on my life. With somewhat impeded speech, she taught me more about being thankful in all circumstances than many with eloquent tongue. Wracked with pain and weakened by the disease that invaded her body, Ali showed me that real strength comes from the inside. She modeled what it looks like to make the Lord your refuge and strength. No doubt she heard the words from her Father in Heaven, "Well done, good and faithful. Well done." I look forward to visiting with Allison again in Glory. Of course then, she won't need help bringing the straw of her water glass to her mouth, or an extra pair of hands to adjust the pillows on her bed. What a day, glorious day that will be. (*Ben was a very special friend to Allison whose weekly visits were met with great anticipation! I bet she can't wait for this next one! *)

Ben DeRegt
Christian Counselor and Teacher
Lynden Christian High School

Ali's journey had been a blessing in many ways, but also had many challenges. I met Ali when my own journey was rocky and missing forgiveness. The one thing that I found In Ali was her wonderful outlook on life and her ability to shine even in her private moments of pain. Her ability to shine and express understanding and forgiveness for others came from a strong belief in Christ and her family. Her warm personality also gave others the ability to feel the wonderful and powerful moments of her life and share in her journey that reached out to touch so many.

She truly had the insight that God wished upon the world.

Her ability to share her journey through the funny and private moments we've shared have truly shaped my own life. She has helped me see that everyone's abilities are different and we all need to work on bringing a positive piece to this world as well as work on our forgiveness with one another. Ali's ability to work on this has brought a positive change into my own world. I know her journey is not completed but has become a wonderful gift for those who have been blessed to know her and continues to miss her.

Lace up those golden sneakers and welcome home dear friend.

"Thank you for painting the rainbow you leave me each day."

William (Bill) Fale

I remember one of my favorite memories that I have of Allison, was on our way back from going to the Northwest Washington Fair ground in August. Not sure the year. Well, on our way back Allison wanted me to drive her wheelchair because she was getting tired of driving it. So I did, and I accidently caused her wheelchair to go right into a tow truck, and she said to me—"that's it....I am taking over right now." One of my other favorite memories of Allison was when I got to spend the night with her at the Christian Health Care Center and staying up late watching movies and talking late in the night. I have one more to tell you about my special time with Allison. We were on our way back to the Christian Health Care Center when her wheelchair happened to go off the sidewalk and it went into a big hole in the ground. I told her to stay there, and I would be right back with a care giver to help. Allison was laughing so hard, while I was panicking. But we did get it out.

Jasmine Lange

Remembering the smile as we picked her up with the special van and always felt lifted up by her spirit and were ministered to us by her. She expressed such joy in worshipping, again remembering that incredible smile. She shared her testimony at church, and it was a powerful time, touching many lives. Her wonderful spirit that brought joy and filled so many of us around her up. Her cup always seemed to be half full, not half empty. Allison blessed us to see the right perspective on life.

Pastor Loren Vonwoudenberg

One of the memories I won't forget, was when Allison and I were on the airplane heading to Disneyland, and she sat right behind me. She said this is my first plane ride, and I hope I don't throw up. She did, but we still had so much fun on that trip and went on several rides together. Ali and I have known each other from the time we were three. We met at Allison's home, where the Whatcom Infant Stimulation Program was first starting. We went through all our schooling together. We both went to camp horizon, where we shared a room, shared camp counselors, and snuck out with them during the night while everyone else was in bed. We went to spin dances together, volunteered at the arc, went to advocacy meetings traveling to Seattle and Olympia. I remember Allison loved to sing, loved to be in the choir, and I think she had a beautiful voice like an angel. I remember we sang together for the "FreeWheelChairMission" fundraiser benefit at Lynden High school. We were both so nervous the mike was shaking in her hand. She wanted me to do it and not her. I told NO, I won't do it for you. She carried her Bible always, and we both came to a saving knowledge of Jesus as our Lord. Allison was eight years old, and I was nine. She would talk about Heaven every and now and then, and give me her rendition of it.

To be sure, we both know its real. And one day I will see Allison again, maybe as neighbors.

Teri Hanson

This comes with a heavy heart, but at the same time a joyous one. For to be absent from the body is to be with the Lord. By all means we know that Allison is dancing in Heaven and praising and worshipping our Lord. The short few years that I had the privilege of being a part of Allison's life were very special. She inspired me and others of her courage and tenacity and will to be all that she could be that the Lord wanted her to be, even with the limitations in her life. Being raised to love God with all her being even through the difficult times showed others that it's not what we have to endure but how we accept and walk through the challenges of life that really counts. To the Lord be all the Glory for giving me the opportunity to see the love of our Lord and Savior through Allison.

Sandy Barstad

Ten years ago in 1999 in the month of July, Allison, my wife Sue and I, & Meredith went down to Seattle to the Individualized Funding conference (quite large… approximately 400 people attending). At one point Meredith had left the room where the conference was being held, and Allison turned to me (Ken) and held my hand and began to share with me… to look at the room and all the participants, with their differing disabilities, and Allison told me that I had a talent to be a voice for the disability community and that I should always continue, never giving up. Because, she said, your voice will speak loudly in the end, to make such a difference for all these people. What a timely word of encouragement. I will never forget that moment, for I went on to become the President of People First of Washington in the year of 2000 to become a strong voice in the advocacy community. I am still actively working in it.

Ken Larson

From the first time we met Allison at Camp Horizon, it was evident to us that God had his hand upon her. Throughout her life, everyone coming in contact with her experienced her steadfast love and observed her faithfulness to the Lord in the midst of the obstacles she faced. Ali was a true friend to our son Derek who was also wheelchair bound. *Both are now rewarded with perfected bodies in their new Heavenly Home!*

Don and Addy Vanden Berg

We can all be God's instrument to demonstrate his love and wisdom when we become humble in spirit. Allison taught us incredible life lessons throughout her time with us here, without ever knowing how lasting and profound those teachings would be. Ali's joyful spirit drew others to her, which allowed her to touch so many in such a short time. With that sparkle in her eye and smile that could melt even the hardest of hearts, she had us all wrapped around her precious little finger!

This is how we'll always remember Allison. A giver of "joy." May we all strive to give as she gave...

Uncle Jamey & Aunt Wanda Evans

Ali was an incredibly patient and positive person. Although we never spoke about it, she clearly understood that this was not her "home" and that she was just passing through. She so valued her relationships! Some of my fondest memories are just sitting and chatting about the day! No matter what, she would flash her fabulous smile that always lit up the room! Ali you are missed! Save me a spot at the banquet table...what a time we will have!

Emily Rogers

Appendix of Scriptures

From Chapter 1

John 10:28 I give them eternal life, and they shall never perish; and no one can snatch them out of my hand.

John 3:16 For God so loved the world that He gave His only Son, that whoever believes in Him shall not perish but have eternal life.

1 Corinthians 1:2 To those everywhere who call on the name of the Lord.

Isaiah 41:10 So do not fear I am with you; do not be dismayed I am your God.

I will strengthen you and help you; I will uphold you with my righteous right hand.

Revelation 21:27 Nothing impure will enter it, nor will anyone who does what is shameful or deceitful, but only those whose names are written in the Lamb's book of life.

2 Corinthians 1:3 Praise be to the God and Father of our Lord Jesus Christ, the Father of compassion, and the Father of all comfort.

Isaiah 9:6 For to us, a child is born, for to us a Son is given, and the government will be upon His shoulders. And He will be called Wonderful Counselor, Mighty God, Everlasting Father, Prince of Peace.

John 14:26 But the Counselor, the Holy Spirit, whom the Father will send in my name, will teach you all things in my name, and will remind you of everything I have said to you.

Luke 5:20 When Jesus saw their faith, He said, "Friend, your sins are forgiven."

Isaiah 55:1 "Come, all of you who are thirsty. Come to the waters, and you who have no money, come buy and eat. Come, buy wine without money and without cost."

Matthew 3:2 He said: "Turn away from your sins, the Kingdom of Heaven is near." NIV

Matthew 4:17 From that time on, Jesus began to preach: "Turn away from your sins." He said. "The Kingdom of Heaven is near." NIV

Acts 17:24 "The God who made this world and everything in it, is the Lord of Heaven and earth, and does not live in temples built by hands."

Hebrews 1:14 Are not all angels ministering spirits sent to serve those who will inherit salvation.

John 14:1-3 "Do not let your hearts be troubled. Trust in God. Trust also in me. Vs 2 "In my Father's house are many rooms; if it were not so, I would have told you. I am going there to prepare a place for you.

Vs 3 And if I go to prepare a place for you, I will come back and take you to be with me, that you also may be where I am."

Revelation 21:1, 3, 4 Then I saw a new Heaven and a new earth, the first Heaven and the first earth had passed away, and there was no longer any sea. Vs 3 And I heard a loud voice from the throne saying, Now the dwelling of God is with men, and He will live with them. They will be his people, and God himself will be with them and be their God. Vs 4 He will wipe every tear from their eyes. There will be no more death, or mourning, or crying or pain, for the old order of things have passed away.

2 Corinthians 5:17 Therefore in anyone is in Christ, He is a new creation, the old has gone, the new has come.

John 6:51 I am the living bread that came down from Heaven.

1Peter 1:3 Then I saw a new Heaven and a new earth, for the first Heaven and the first earth had passed away, and there was no longer any sea.

Psalm 23:6 Surely goodness and love will follow me all the days of my life, and I will dwell in the house of the LORD forever.

John 3:16 For God so loved the world that He gave His one and only Son, that whoever believes in Him shall not perish, but have everlasting life.

John 10:7 Therefore Jesus said again, I tell you the truth, I am the gate for the sheep.

John 14:6 Jesus answered, I am the way, the truth, the life. No one comes through the Father except through me.

Hebrews 16:9 We have this hope as an anchor for the soul, firm and secure.

1 Peter 1:4 and unto an inheritance that can never perish, spoil or fade — kept in Heaven for you.

Hebrews 1:3 The Son is the radiance of God's glory the exact representation of His being, sustaining all things by His powerful word. After He had provided purification for all sins, He sat down at the right hand of the Majesty in Heaven.

Isaiah 51:1 "Listen to me, you who pursue righteousness and who seek the LORD, look to the rock from which you were cut and to the quarry from which you were hewn.

John 11:25, 26 Jesus said to her, "I am the resurrection and the life. He who believes in me will live, even though He dies. Vs 26 and whoever lives and believes in me will never die. Do you believe this?

John 14:6 Jesus answered, "I am the way, the truth, and the life. No one comes through the Father except through me."

From Chapter 2

Hebrews 11:16 They were longing for a better country, a heavenly one. Therefore God is not ashamed to be called their God, for He has prepared a city for them.

Psalm 23:4 Even though I walk through the valley of the shadow of death, I will fear no evil for you are with me; your rod and your staff they comfort me.

2 Corinthians 5:8 Absent from the body and at home with the Lord.

1 Peter 1:4 In His great mercy, he has given us new birth into a living hope, through the resurrection of Jesus

Christ, and into an inheritance that can never perish, spoil or fade—kept in heaven for you.

Isaiah 51:12 I even I, am He who comforts you.

Hebrews 12:2 Let us fix our eyes on Jesus the author and perfecter of our faith, who for the joy set before him, endured the cross scorning its shame, and sat down at the right hand of the throne of God.

Romans 12:2 Do not conform any longer to the pattern of this world, but be transformed by the renewing of your mind.

Luke 23:43 Jesus answered him, "I tell you the truth, today you will be with me in paradise."

2 Corinthians 5:7 We walk by faith, not by sight.

Revelation 7:7 All the angels were standing around the throne and around the elders and the four living creatures. They fell down on their faces and worshipped God.

Revelation 21:22 I did not see a temple in the city, because the Lord God Almighty and the Lamb are its temple.

John 11:25-26 Jesus said to her: "I am the resurrection and the life. He who believes in me will live, even though he dies;

26 and whoever lives and believes in me will never die. Do you believe this?"

From Chapter 3

Jeremiah 1:5 Before I formed you in the womb I knew you, before you were born I set you apart.

Isaiah 44:2 This is what the Lord says—He who made you, who formed you in the womb, and who will help you.

Isaiah 44:24 This is what the Lord says—your redeemer who formed you in the womb. I am the Lord who has made all things who alone stretched out the heavens, and spread out the earth by myself.

Jeremiah 1:5 Before I formed you in the womb I knew you, before you were born I set you apart and appointed you as a prophet to the nations.

Psalm 139:13 For you created my inmost being; you knit me together in my mother's womb. I am fearfully and wonderfully made, your eyes saw my unformed body. All the days ordained for me were written in your book before one of them came to be.

Ephesians 2:10 For we are God's workmanship, created in Christ Jesus to do good works, which God prepared in advance for us to do.

Colossians 3:3 your life is now hidden with Christ in God.

From Chapter 4

Isaiah 51:13 The Lord your maker, who stretched out the heavens, and laid the foundations of the earth.

Psalm 147:4 He determines the numbers of the stars and calls them each by name.

Isaiah 40:26 Lift your eyes and look to the heavens: Who created all these? He who brings out the starry host one by one, and calls them each by name.

Because of His great power and mighty strength, not one of them is missing.

Psalm 139: 1-2 Oh Lord, you have searched me and you know me.

2 You know when I sit and when I arise, you perceive my thoughts from afar.

Isaiah 40:22, 26 He sits enthroned above the circle of the earth, and its people are like grasshoppers. He stretches out the heavens like a canopy, and spreads them out like a tent to live in.

Romans 12:2 Do not conform any longer to the pattern of this world, but be transformed by the renewing of your mind. Then you will be able to test and approve what God's will is.

1 John 4:8 Whoever does not love does not know God, because God is love.

Ephesians 1:5 He predestined us to be adopted as his sons through Jesus Christ, in accordance with his pleasure and will.

Ephesians 2:10 For we are God's workmanship, created in Christ Jesus, to do good works, which God prepared in advance for us to do.

Romans 8:23 We wait eagerly for the adoption as sons, the redemption of our bodies.

Psalm 139: 15-16 My frame was not hidden from you when I was made in the secret place. When I was woven together in the depths of the earth,

16. your eyes saw my unformed body. All the days ordained for me were written in your book before one of them came to be.

Ephesians 2:10 For we are God's workmanship, created in Christ Jesus to do good works, which God prepared in advance for us to do.

Jeremiah 31:3 The Lord appeared unto us in the past saying: "I have loved you with an everlasting love; I have drawn you with everlasting kindness."

Genesis 1:26 Then God said, "Let us make man in our image, in our likeness, and let them rule over the fish of the sea and the birds of the air, over the livestock, over the earth, and over the creatures that lie along the ground."

Psalm 139:16 And your eyes saw my unformed body. All the days ordained for me were written in your book, before one of them came to be.

Luke 12:7 Indeed, the very hairs of your head are numbered. Don't be afraid; you are worth more than many sparrows.

Matthew 10:30 And even the very hairs on your head are numbered.

Revelation 22:12 Behold I am coming soon. My reward is with me, and I will give to everyone according to what he has done.

Psalm 139: 3-4 You discern my going out, and my lying down; you are familiar with all my ways.

4. Before a word is on my tongue, you know it completely, O Lord.

Romans 8:28 And we know that in all things God works for the good of those who love him, who have been called according to his purpose.

Jeremiah 29:11 For I know the plans I have for you, "declares the Lord', plans to prosper you and not to harm you, plans to give you a hope and a future. Colossians 1:10 and we pray this in order that you may live a life worthy or the Lord and please Him in every way: bearing fruit in every good work, growing in the knowledge of God.

Colossians 3: 2-4 Set your mind on things above, not on earthly things.

3. For you died, and your life is now hidden with Christ in God.

4. When Christ, who is your life, appears, then you will also appear with Him in glory.

Psalm 139:5 You hem me in behind and before; you have laid your hand upon me.

John 15:16 You did not choose me, but I choose you to go and appointed you to bear fruit — fruit that will last. Then the Father will give you whatever you ask in my name.

1 Peter 1:18 For you know that it was not with perishable things such as silver or gold that you were redeemed from the empty way of life handed down to you from your forefathers.

Jeremiah 31:3 I have loved you with an everlasting love, I have drawn you with loving kindness.

Mark 1:14 Jesus went into Galilee proclaiming the good news of God.

Isaiah 55: 1, 6 Come all you who are thirsty, come to the waters; and you who have no money, come bye and eat. Come bye wine and milk without money and without cost.

6 Seek the Lord while He may be found; call on Him while He is near.

Revelation 3:20 Here I am. I stand at the door and knock. If anyone hears my voice and opens the door, I will come in and eat with him, and he with me.

Hebrews 11:6 And without faith its impossible to believe God, because anyone who comes to Him, must believe that He exists, and that He rewards those who earnestly seek Him.

From Chapter 5

Genesis 1:26 Then God said: "Let us make man in our image and our likeness and let them rule over the fish of the sea, and the birds of the air, over the livestock, over all the earth, and over all the creatures that move along the ground."

Genesis 1:28 God blessed them and said to them: "Be fruitful and increase in number; fill the earth and subdue it. Rule over the fish of the sea and the birds of the air and over every living creature that moves on the ground."

Genesis 2:1 Thus the Heavens and the earth were completed in all their vast array.

Genesis 2:3 And God rested from all the work of creating that He had done.

Genesis 2:4 This is the account of the Heavens and the earth when they were created.

Genesis 2:8 Now the LORD God has planted a garden in the east, in Eden, and there He put the man He had formed.

9. And the LORD God made all kinds of trees grow out of the ground — trees that were pleasing to the eye and good for food. In the middle of the garden were the tree of life and the tree of the knowledge of good and evil.

Genesis 2: 15-17 The LORD God took the man and put him in the Garden of Eden to work it and take care of it.

16. and the LORD God commanded the man, "You are free to eat from any tree in the garden;

17. but you must not eat from the tree of the knowledge of good and evil, for when you eat of it you shall surely die."

Romans 5:14 Nevertheless, death reigned from the time of Adam.

Genesis 2:7 the Lord God formed the man from the dust of the ground and breathed into his nostrils the breath of life, the man became a living being.

Genesis chapter 3: "The Fall of Man" — where our inherited sin nature began.

Genesis 3:1-24 Now the serpent was more crafty than any of the wild animals the Lord God had made. He said to the women, "Did God really say, 'You must not eat from any tree in the garden'? "

2. The woman said to the serpent, "We may eat fruit from the trees in the garden,

3. but God did say, 'you must not eat fruit from the tree that is in the middle of the garden, and you must not touch it, or you will die.'"

4. "You will not surely die," the serpent said to the woman.

5. "For God knows that when you eat of it your eyes will be opened, and you will be like God, knowing good and evil."

6. When the woman saw that the fruit of the tree was good for good and pleasing to the eye, and also desirable for gaining wisdom, she took some and ate it. She also gave some to her husband, who was with her, and he ate it.

7. Then the eyes of both of them were opened, and they realized they were naked; so they sewed fig leaves together and made coverings for themselves.

8. Then the man and his wife heard the sound of the Lord God as he was walking in the garden in the cool of the day, and they hid from the Lord God among the trees of the garden.

9. But the Lord God called to the man," Where are you?"

10. He answered, "I heard you in the garden, and I was afraid because I was naked, so I hid."

11. And he said, "Who told you that you were naked? Have you eaten from the tree that I commanded you not to eat from?"

12. The man said, "The woman you put here with me — she gave me some fruit from the tree, and I ate it."

13. Then the Lord God said to the woman, "What is this you have done?" The woman said, "The serpent deceived me, and I ate."

14. So the Lord God said to the serpent, "Because you have done this, "Cursed are you above all the livestock and all the wild animals. You will crawl on your belly and you will eat dust all the days of your life.

15. And I will put enmity between you and the woman, and between our offspring and hers; he will crush your head, and you will strike his heel."

16. To the woman he said, "I will greatly increase your pains in childbearing; with pain you will give birth to children. Your desire will be for you husband, and he will rule over you."

17. To Adam he said, "Because you listened to your wife and ate from the tree about which I commanded you, 'You must not eat of it,'

"Cursed is the ground because of you; through painful toil you will eat of it All the days of your life.

18. It will produce thorns and thistles for you, and you will eat the plants of the field.

19. By the sweat of your brow you will eat your food until you return to the ground, since from it you were taken; for dust you are and to dust you will return."

20. Adam named his wife Eve, because she would become the mother of all the living.

21. The Lord God made garments of skin for Adam and his wife and clothed them.

22 And the Lord God said, "The man has now become like one of us, knowing good and evil. He must not be allowed to reach our hand and take also from the tree of life and eat, and live forever."

23. So the Lord God banished him from the Garden of Eden to work the ground from which he had been taken.

24. After he drove the man out, he placed on the east side of the Garden of Eden cherubim and a flaming sword flashing back and forth to guard the way to the tree of life.

Romans 5:6 You see, at just the right time, when we were still powerless Christ died for the ungodly. Romans 8:3 For what the law was powerless to do in that it was weakened by the (curse) the sinful nature, God did by sending His own Son in the likeness of sinful man to be a sin offering. And so He condemned sin in sinful man.

4. In order that the righteous requirements of the law might be fully met in us, who do not live according to the sinful nature but according to the Spirit.

Ephesians 4:17 -19 So I tell you this, and insist on it in the Lord, that you must no longer live as the Gentiles do, in the futility of their thinking.

18. They are darkened in their understanding and separated from the life of God because of the ignorance that is in them due to the hardening of their hearts.

19. Having lost all sensitivity, they have given themselves over to sensuality, so as to indulge in every kind of impurity, with a continual lust for more.

1 Corinthians 13:12 Now we see a poor reflection as in a mirror; then we shall see face to face. Now I know in part; then I shall know fully, even as I am fully known.

Genesis 3:15 I will put enmity between you and the woman, and between her offspring and hers; he will crush your head and you will strike his heel.

John 3:16 For God so loved the world that He gave his one and only Son, so that whoever believes in him shall not perish, but have eternal life.

Ephesians 2:12 Remember that at that time, you were separate from Christ, excluded from citizenship in Israel and foreigners to the covenants of the promise, without hope and without God in the world.

Galatians 4:7 So you are no longer a slave, but a son; and since you are a son, God has made you also an heir.

2 Samuel 4:4 Jonathan son of Saul had a son who was lame in both feet. He was five years old when the news about Saul and Jonathan came from Jezreel. His nurse picked Him up and fled, but as she hurried to leave, he fell and became crippled. His name was Mephibosheth.

1 Samuel 20:13-15 But if my father (Saul) is inclined to harm you (David), may the LORD deal with me, be it ever so severely, if I do not let you know and send you away safely. May the LORD be with you as He has been with my Father.

14. But show me unfailing kindness like that of the LORD as long as I live, so that I may not be killed,

15. and do not ever cut off your kindness from my family — not even when the LORD has cut off every one of David's enemies from the face of the earth.

2 Samuel 9:1 David asked. "Is there anyone still left of the house of Saul to whom I can show kindness for Jonathan's sake?

2 Samuel 9:7 "Don't be afraid," David said to him, "for I will surely show you kindness for the sake of your Father

Jonathan. I will restore to you all the land that belonged to your grandfather Saul, and you will always eat at my table."

Revelation 3:20 I will come in and eat (sup) with him, and He with me.

From Chapter 6

John 10:11 I am the good shepherd. The shepherd lays down his life for his sheep.

John 10:18 I have authority to lay it down and authority to take it up again.

Philippians 3:20 But our citizenship is in heaven. And we eagerly await a Savior from there, the Lord Jesus Christ, who by the power that enables him to bring everything under his control, will transform our lowly bodies so that they will be like his glorious body.

2 Peter 1:4 Through these he has given us his great and precious promises, so that through them you may partici-

pate in the divine nature and escape the corruption in the world caused by evil desires.

Ephesians 2:1, 8, 12, 13 As for you, you were dead in your tresses passes and sins.

8. For it is by grace that you have been saved, — through faith, and this not from yourselves, it is the gift of God.

12. Remember that at the time, you were separate from Christ, excluded from citizenship in Israel and foreigners to the covenants of the promise, without hope and without God in the world.

13. But now in Christ Jesus you who once were far away have been brought near through the blood of Christ.

Titus 3:4-8 But when the kindness of God our Savior and His love for mankind appeared,

5. He saved us, not on the basis of deeds which we have done in righteousness, but according to His mercy, by the washing of regeneration and renewing by the Holy Spirit.

6. whom He poured out upon us richly through Jesus Christ our Savior,

7. so that being justified by His grace we would be made heirs according to the hope of eternal life.

8. This is a trustworthy statement.

Romans 6:10 For if, by the trespass of one man, death reigned through that one man, how much more will those who receive God's abundant provision of Grace, and of the gift of righteousness, reign if life through the one man Jesus Christ.

Hebrews 1:10 He also says, "In the beginning, O Lord, you laid the foundations of the earth, and the heavens are the works of your hands."

Colossians 1:22 But now, he has reconciled you by Christ's physical body through death to present you holy in his sight, without blemish, and free from accusation.

Romans 8: 1 Therefore, there is now no condemnation for those who are in Christ Jesus, because through Christ Jesus the law of the Spirit of life, set me free from the law of sin and death. Genesis 3: The Fall recorded: Found on page 46, chapter five.

Ephesians 2:8, 9, 10 For it is by grace that you have been saved, through faith, — and this, not from yourselves, it is the gift of God, —

9. not by works, so that no one can boast.

10. For we are God's workmanship, created in Christ Jesus to do good works, which God prepared in advance for us to do.

Romans 6:10 The death He died, He dies to sin once for all; but the life he lives, he lives to God.

2 Corinthians 5:17 Therefore, if anyone is in Christ, he is a new creation; the old has gone the new has come.

2 Peter 1:4 Through these he has given us his great and precious promises, so that through them you may participate in the divine nature and escape the corruption in the world caused by evil desires.

Revelation 3:20 Here I am. I stand at the door and knock. If anyone hears my voice and opens the door, I will come in and eat with him, and he with me.

From Chapter 7

John 14:1-3 Do not let your hearts be troubled. Trust in God; trust also in me.

2. In my Father's house are many rooms; if it were not so, I woul have told you. I am going there to prepare a place for you.

3. And if I go and prepare a place for you, I will come back and take you to be with me that you also may be with me where I am.

Revelation 4:3 And the one who sat there had the appearance of jasper and carnelian. A rainbow, resembling an emerald, encircled the throne.

1 Peter 1:4 and into an inheritance that can never perish, spoil, or fade—kept in Heaven for you.

Revelation 1:18 I am the Living One; I was dead, and behold I am alive for ever and ever! And I hold the keys of death and Hades.

About Free Wheelchair Mission

‹⸱⸱⸱⸱⸱⸱›

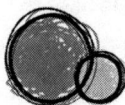

Free Wheelchair Mission®
TRANSFORMING LIVES THROUGH THE GIFT OF MOBILITY

Their mission is to transform lives through the gift of mobility to the physically disabled poor in developing countries as motivated by Jesus Christ. Their vision is to provide 20 million wheelchairs. Founded in 2001, Free Wheelchair Mission is an international non profit organization dedicated to providing wheelchairs to the disabled poor in developing nations.

Proceeds from the sales of this book will go to funding these light weight chairs.

www.Freewheelchairmission.org

Years ago, Don and Laurie Schoendorfer were vacationing in Morocco when they witnessed the plight of a disabled woman struggling to drag herself across a dirt road. Ignored by the crowds and barely evading traffic, the woman's hardship was a scene the couple would be unable to forget upon their return to life in southern California.

Don was a Columbia University graduate with a Ph.D. in engineering from MIT, working in the biomedical field, and responsible for a string of over 50 U.S. patents. Because of his passion for serving the poor, he eventually walked away from a successful career in research and development and developed the inexpensive and durable wheelchair that would become the heart and soul of Free Wheelchair Mission.

Don launched Free Wheelchair Mission with a handful of prototype chairs packed along on a mission trip to India in 2001. When he lifted a child into the first chair, Don realized that God had created a path for him, and the Free Wheelchair Mission was born. The humanitarian organization would grow to distribute over **544,950 wheelchairs to 77 countries to date, January 2011** with a goal of eventually reaching 20 million of the world's disabled population. **$59.20** can change a life.

In March of 2008, Don was awarded the *"Above and Beyond Award"* by the Congressional Medal of Honor Society for his work among the disabled poor, one of the first civilians ever to receive this accolade. *www. freewheelchairmission.org*

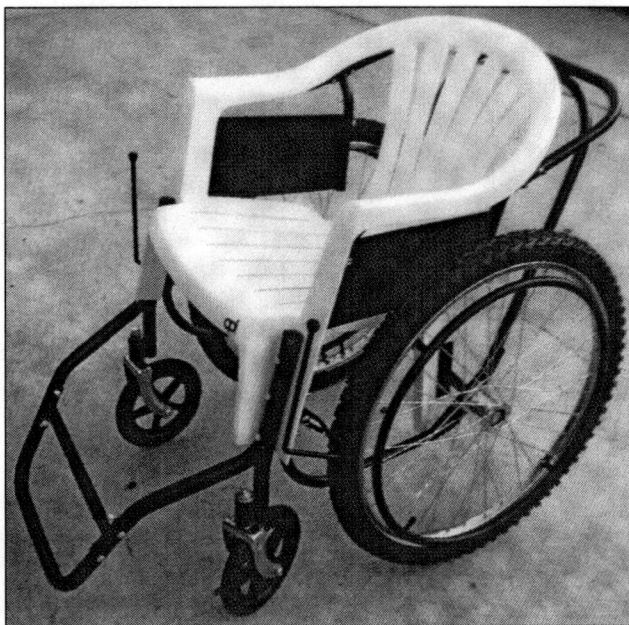

LaVergne, TN USA
10 March 2011
219577LV00001B/1/P